Creative Kids Math

GRADES 1–2

S0-BCN-910

Brighter Child®
An imprint of Carson-Dellosa Publishing LLC
Greensboro, North Carolina

Brighter Child®
An imprint of Carson-Dellosa Publishing LLC
P.O. Box 35665
Greensboro, NC 27425 USA

Printed in the USA • All rights reserved.   ISBN 978-1-62057-659-5
01-002131151

Table of Contents

Introduction

Every day, your child encounters math in many different situations. The activities in *Creative Kids Math* make learning math skills fun no matter what he or she is doing!

In this book, your child will:

- Read a story about Max and Emma and practice math skills by measuring rain in a tracker and telling time.

- Play fun math games that help your child with addition, subtraction, shapes, and critical thinking.

- Learn about liquids, solids, gases, weather, and space—which helps your child graph observations, measure and classify, and use halves and wholes in experiments.

- Create a snowy masterpiece using different shapes, stamp half and whole pieces of fruit to create a fraction collage, and mix a bubble recipe to count and pop as many bubbles as possible.

The Secret Code

It was a rainy day. Max and Emma could not play outside. Emma was at home in her science lab.

"Let's see how much it has rained," Emma said. "I bet my rain tracker is almost full!"

The phone rang. "Emma! Max is on the phone," her mom called.

Directions: Fill up the rain tracker. Use the ruler to color 3 inches of rain.

"Hi Max," Emma said.

"Hi Emma," Max said. "I put something secret in your mailbox."

"What is it?" Emma asked.

"You will see," Max said. "Once you solve it, put it in my mailbox."

"Okay, I will check now!" Emma said. She grabbed an umbrella and went outside.

Directions: Color the picture.

Back inside, Emma opened the letter. It was written in a secret code. "Cool!" Emma said. "Max made his own code." She looked at the key. "I see, each symbol stands for a letter," she said.

"I need to check my rain tracker first," Emma said. But it had stopped raining outside.

"I have the perfect message for Max!" Emma said as she started writing.

Directions: What will Emma do after she writes the code? Draw what happens next below.

"I wish we could play outside," Max sighed.
The phone rang.

"Hello?" Max said.

"Go check your mailbox!" Emma said.

"I'll go right now!" Max said.

Directions: Help Max solve the code from Emma.
Use the key to unlock the message.

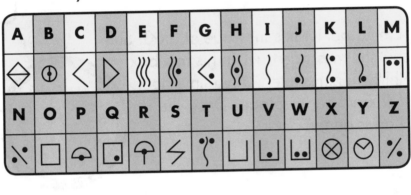

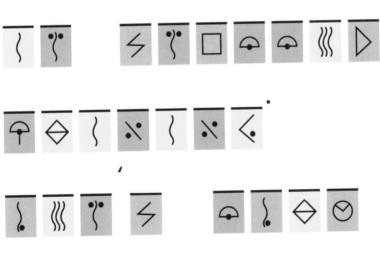

Directions: Write your answers on the lines.

How many inches of rain does Emma collect on page 7?

_____ inches

Emma got Max's message at 3:00. She put the message back in his mailbox thirty minutes later. What time does Max get her message? Draw the hands on the clock.

Use a ruler to find something around your house that measures 3 inches. Draw it below.

Make your own rain tracker on page 74!

5 − 2 = _____3_____

Ordinal Numbers: Birthday Balloons

Max and Emma are at a birthday party! Which balloon will they pick? Look at the balloons and follow the directions.

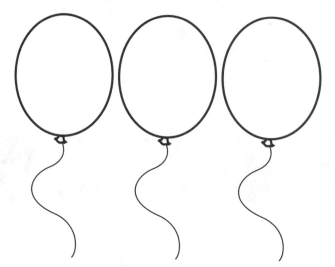

Directions: Color the **second** balloon **red**.

Draw **blue** and **green** stripes on the **first** balloon.

Draw an animal on the **third** balloon.

Ordinal Numbers: Ice Cream Dilemma

Max and Emma love ice cream. Help them decide which ice cream cone to eat first and which to eat last.

Directions: Draw a line to the picture that matches the ordinal number in the left column.

eighth

third

sixth

ninth

seventh

second

fourth

first

fifth

tenth

More Than

The symbol > means **more than**. It is written like this: **7 > 5**.

Directions: Count the grapes. Write the numbers on the lines. Use the symbol > to write which bunch has more.

_____ ◯ _____

Less Than

The symbol < means **less than**. It is written like this: **6 < 7**.

Directions: Count the seeds on the watermelon. Draw less seeds on the watermelon below it.

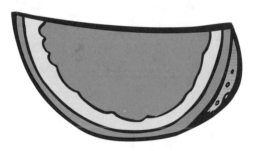

Directions: Fill in the number of seeds you drew on the line below. Then, write the math symbol that means **less than**.

_____ ◯ 9

Crazy for Bananas!

The monkeys at the zoo eat a lot of bananas. Which monkey eats more?

Directions: Count the bananas. Circle the monkey that eats more. Write the missing math symbol in the circle.

8 ◯ 5

Directions: Write the missing math symbol in each circle.

18 ◯ 15   20 ◯ 12

4 ◯ 6   2 ◯ 1

10 ◯ 5   14 ◯ 13

Apple Addition

Addition means putting together or adding two or more numbers. When you add two numbers together, you get a **total** or **sum**.

Directions: Count the apples and write how many.

+ = _____

+ = _____

+ = _____

+ = _____

Addition

Directions: The key words **in all** tell you to add. Circle the key words **in all** and solve the problem.

A monster has 4 yellow shoes and 2 red shoes. How many shoes does the monster have in all?

4 $\bigcirc$ 2 = _____

Now, draw the monster wearing all the shoes.

Emma's Addition

Emma loves addition! Help Max solve the math problems she wrote for him. Then, create your own addition problem for a friend.

Directions: Add the numbers.

8	2	3	5	4
+ 1	+ 5	+ 7	+ 4	+ 1

9	5	2	5	6
+ 1	+ 3	+ 2	+ 5	+ 0

Directions: Create your own problem. Give it to a friend to solve.

_____ + _____ = _____

Spaceship Addition

Directions: Add the numbers. Write each answer on the spaceship.

2 + 4 =

1 + 3 =

3 + 2 =

5 + 1 =

2 + 2 =

6 + 2 =

4 + 6 =

2 + 7 =

Addition Problem Solving

Directions: Solve each problem. Show your work.

There are 4 .

5 more come.

Now, how many are here? _____

There are 5 .

There are 6 .

How many and in all? _____

Jenny has 5 🌼 .

She finds 2 more 🌼 .

What is the sum of 5 + 2? _____

Subtraction

Subtraction means taking away or subtracting one number from another. The symbol used for subtraction is called a **minus sign** (–). It means to subtract the second number from the first.

Directions: Solve the number problem under each picture. Write how much fruit is left.

5 – 2 = _____

7 – 3 = _____

3 – 2 = _____

6 – 1 = _____

Butterfly Scramble

Emma wants to study butterflies in her science lab. But they keep flying away! Help catch the butterflies.

Directions: Circle the key word **left**. Write a number sentence to solve each subtraction problem.

Emma put 6 butterflies in her jar. But 2 flew out. How many butterflies are left in the jar?

_____ – _____ = _____

There were 10 butterflies in a tree. Then, 9 flew into a bush. How many butterflies were left in the tree?

_____ – _____ = _____

Max saw 15 butterflies. He caught 8 of them. How many butterflies does Max have left to catch?

_____ – _____ = _____

Directions: Draw a picture of Max and Emma chasing the butterflies.

Max's Subtraction

Max loves subtraction! Help Emma solve the math problems he wrote for her. Then, create your own subtraction problem for a friend.

Directions: Subtract to find the difference.

$$\begin{array}{r} 10 \\ -7 \\ \hline \end{array} \qquad \begin{array}{r} 9 \\ -5 \\ \hline \end{array} \qquad \begin{array}{r} 4 \\ -3 \\ \hline \end{array} \qquad \begin{array}{r} 2 \\ -0 \\ \hline \end{array} \qquad \begin{array}{r} 9 \\ -3 \\ \hline \end{array}$$

$$\begin{array}{r} 6 \\ -2 \\ \hline \end{array} \qquad \begin{array}{r} 8 \\ -6 \\ \hline \end{array} \qquad \begin{array}{r} 10 \\ -6 \\ \hline \end{array} \qquad \begin{array}{r} 7 \\ -2 \\ \hline \end{array} \qquad \begin{array}{r} 8 \\ -7 \\ \hline \end{array}$$

Directions: Create your own problem. Give it to a friend to solve.

_____ – _____ = _____

Subtraction: Pond Problems

Directions: Complete the subtraction sentences.

4 – 4 = _____

10 – 2 = _____

7 – 3 = _____

6 – 5 = _____

8 – 3 = _____

5 – 2 = _____

Subtraction Problem Solving

Directions: Solve each problem. Show your work. The first one is done for you.

There are 7 .

$$\begin{array}{r} 7 \\ -4 \\ \hline \end{array}$$

4 swim away.

How many are left? _____3_____

Brian wants 10 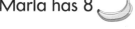.

He has 3 .

What is the difference? _____

Marla has 8 .

She gives 4 🍌 away.

What is 8 – 4? _____

There are 7 🎈.

2 🎈 pop.

How many are left? _____

Shapes and Colors

circle triangle square rectangle

Directions: Color the circles **blue**. Color the triangles **green**. Color the squares **purple**. Color the rectangles yellow.

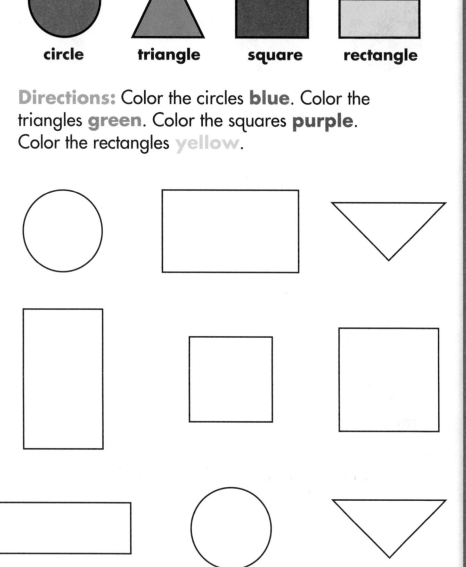

Classifying: Shapes

Directions: Look at the shapes. Answer the questions.

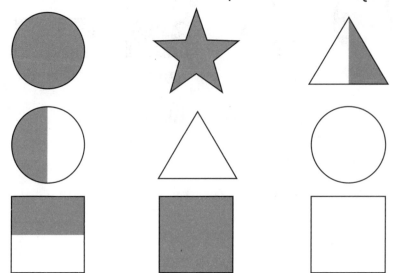

How many all white shapes? _____

How many all **green** shapes? _____

How many half **green** shapes? _____

How many all **green** stars? _____

How many all white circles? _____

How many half white shapes? _____

Fractions

How many equal parts? _____

 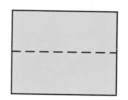 

Directions: Color the shapes with two equal parts.

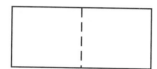 

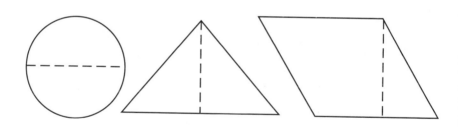

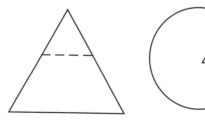 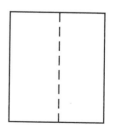

Fractions: Thirds and Fourths

Directions: Each object has three equal parts. Color one part.

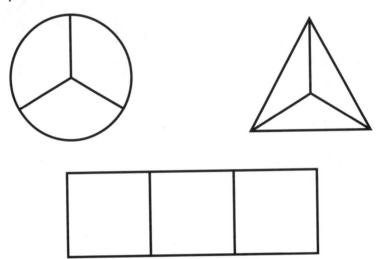

Directions: Each object has four equal parts. Color one part.

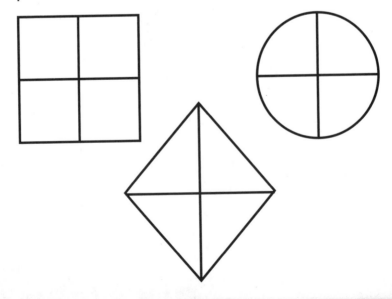

Cupcake Craze!

Emma wants to share eight cupcakes with four friends. If she divides the cupcakes equally, how many will everyone have?

Directions: Draw the cupcakes on the plates to show how many each of Emma's friends gets.

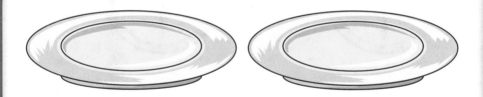

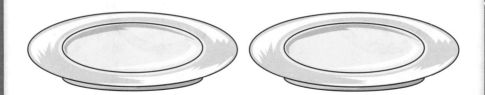

Time: Half Hour

The little hand of the clock tells the hour. The big hand tells how many minutes after the hour. When the minute hand is on the 6, it is on the half hour. A half hour is 30 minutes. It is written :30, such as 5:30.

Directions: Look at each clock. Write the time.

_____ : _____   _____ : _____

_____ : _____   _____ : _____

_____ : _____   _____ : _____

Your Schedule

Directions: Look at the time on the clocks. Write the time. Then, draw a picture of something you do at that time.

_____ : _____

_____ : _____

_____ : _____

Max's Pennies

Max is counting his pennies. A penny  is worth one cent. It is written **1 ¢**.

Directions: Count Max's pennies. How many cents?

 = _____ ¢

 = _____ ¢

= _____ ¢

 = _____ ¢

Count the Change

Max and Emma want to buy ice cream. Help them count their change. A nickel  is worth five cents. It is written **5¢**.

Directions: Count the money and write the answers.

 = _____ ¢

= _____ ¢

= _____ ¢

= _____ ¢

Measurement: Length and Height

Directions: Use dimes to measure each object.

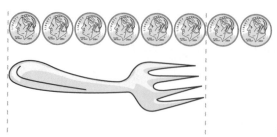

_____ dimes

_____ dimes

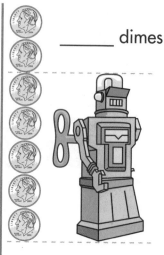

_____ dimes

_____ dimes

_____ dimes

_____ dimes

Measurement: Weight

Emma is experimenting with weight. She is weighing objects she found in her lab. Help her find the heavier and lighter objects.

Directions: Circle the heavier object.

Directions: Circle the lighter object.

Picture Graph

Directions: Time to set the table! Use the picture graph to answer the questions.

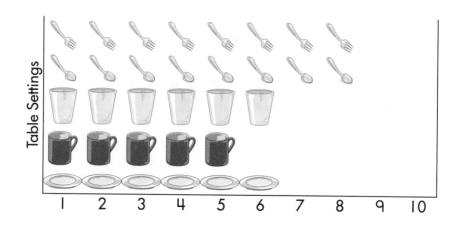

Table Settings

| 1 | 2 | 3 | 4 | 5 | 6 | 7 | 8 | 9 | 10 |

How many more than ? _____

Circle the object that is greater than .

Circle the object that is less than .

Circle the object that is equal to .

Math Games

Number Recognition

Directions: Use the color code to color the parrot.

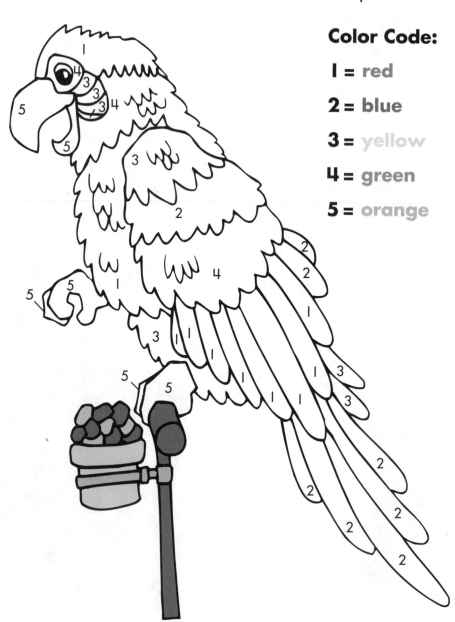

Color Code:

1 = red

2 = blue

3 = yellow

4 = green

5 = orange

Shape Sudoku

Directions: Complete the Sudoku puzzle. Every row and column must contain a ○, ■, ▲, and ♥. Do not repeat the same shape twice in any row or column.

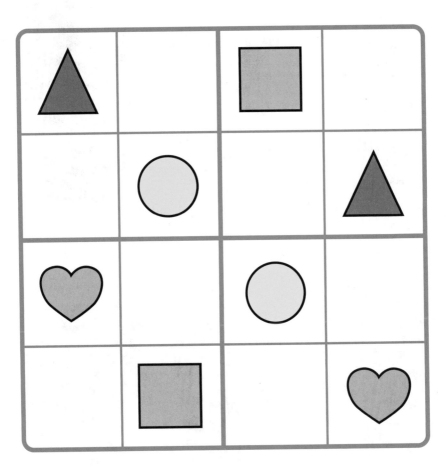

Which Is Different?

Directions: Look at the pictures below. One is different from the others. Draw an **X** on the picture that is different.

Number Word Search

Directions: Find the number words zero through twelve hidden in the box. Words can be across or down.

zero	three	six	nine	twelve
one	four	seven	ten	
two	five	eight	eleven	

```
t e a z w z x a b i g t e n
o l z r b e r e v e d l a j
t w e l v e a b o n e c d z
i a r p q d p s u j x e i w
c f o p l s c k i q u i i o
m s t f v i o e t t f g h d
t n u w x g z w h g h r o
n i n e k f d f o u r t j f
a s g l q c w k o s n v m i
n y c e b o n h h p o m p v
b e x v s s e v e n w e n e
t h r e e r t a l j k x q z
m o a n e n i m u t w a y x
```

Addition and Subtraction: Crack the Code

Directions: Add or subtract the problems. Then, use your answer and the key to write the correct letter on the line above the problem. The first one is done for you.

What is an alien's favorite sweet treat?

M
5
+4
9

  7
+5

 12
− 6

 10
− 7

  5
+3

  8
+4

  9
− 5 −

 15
− 6

 14
− 2

  2
+3

 11
− 6

 14
− 7

  4
+6

 10
− 9 !

Key:

$\frac{M}{9}$	$\frac{A}{12}$	$\frac{L}{5}$	$\frac{S}{1}$	$\frac{W}{10}$
$\frac{N}{4}$	$\frac{R}{6}$	$\frac{I}{8}$	$\frac{T}{3}$	$\frac{O}{7}$

44

Hidden Picture

Directions: There are five things hidden in Emma's lab. Find and circle them. Can you count to **100** by **5**s?

pencil   apple   hat   candy   rock

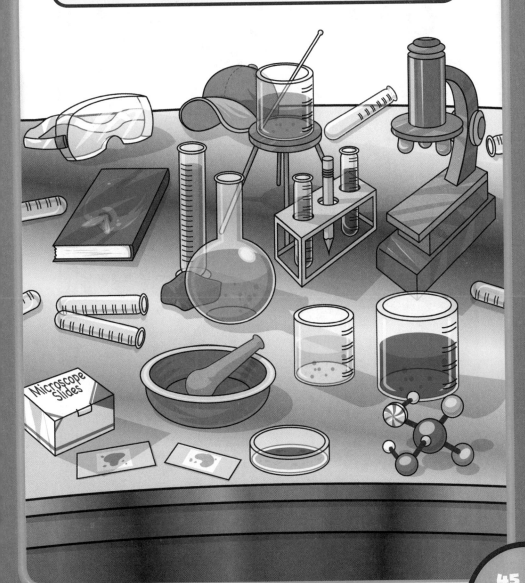

Maze

Directions: Follow the number pattern **13535** to help the fish find its home.

Addition: Color Code

Directions: Add to find the sum. Use the code to color the picture.

Color Code:
1 = red   3 = black   5 = brown
2 = yellow   4 = blue   6 = green

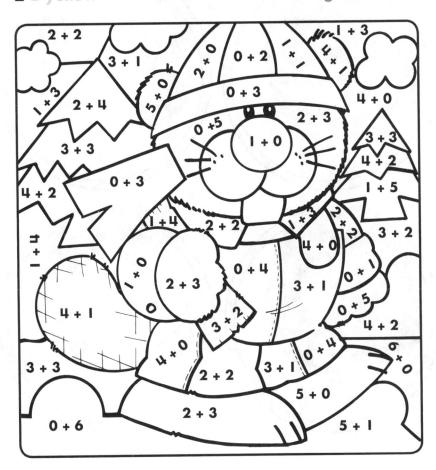

2 + 2   3 + 1   2 + 0   0 + 2   1 + 1   1 + 3   4 + 1   1 + 3   2 + 4   5 + 0   0 + 3   4 + 0   2 + 3   3 + 3   4 + 2   0 + 5   1 + 0   3 + 3   4 + 2   1 + 5   0 + 3   4 + 2   1 + 4   2 + 2   1 + 3   2 + 2   3 + 2   4 + 1   1 + 0   2 + 3   0 + 4   4 + 0   3 + 1   0 + 1   0 + 5   4 + 1   4 + 1   0   3 + 2   4 + 2   6 + 0   3 + 3   4 + 0   2 + 2   3 + 1   0 + 4   5 + 0   0 + 6   2 + 3   5 + 1

Matching Emma

Directions: Find and circle the two pictures of Emma that are exactly alike.

Number Search

Directions: Find the hidden numbers from the box below. They may be hidden across or down.

16177	33899	46437
37269	16396	77468
89448	97987	76373

```
4  6  4  3  7  1  6  3  9  6
1  3  2  5  7  8  2  6  4  1
0  3  5  1  4  2  3  9  0  8
4  8  7  1  6  1  7  7  6  2
2  9  1  7  8  3  2  8  5  7
5  9  4  9  0  2  6  1  4  6
3  1  7  3  9  7  9  8  7  3
5  2  0  2  1  4  2  6  3  7
7  8  9  4  4  8  3  4  5  3
0  4  1  6  2  3  9  2  7  1
```

Which Is Different?

Directions: Look at the aliens below. One is different from the others. Draw an **X** on the alien that is different.

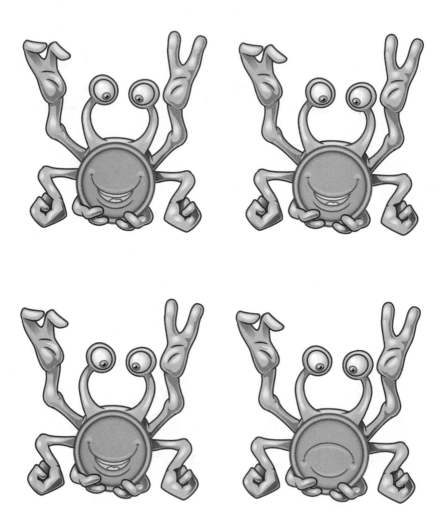

Sudoku

Directions: Complete the Sudoku puzzle. Every row and column must contain the numbers **1**, **2**, **3**, and **4**. Do not repeat the same number twice in any row or column.

	1	4	
4			2
1			4
	4	2	

Color Code: Shapes

Directions: Color the squares **green**, rectangles **yellow**, circles **red**, and triangles **blue**.

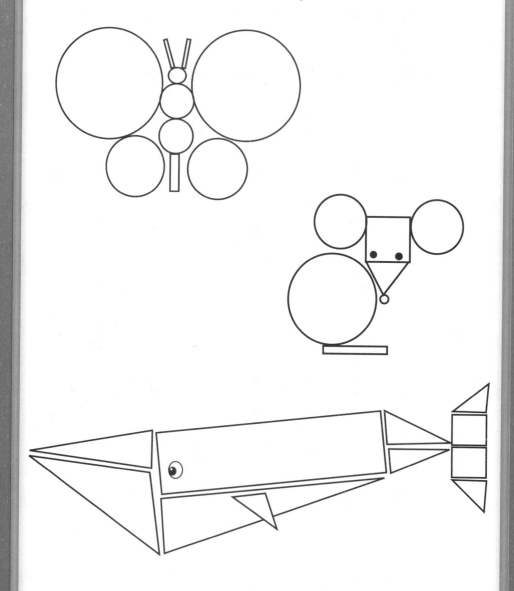

Color Code

Directions: Subtract to find the answers. Use the code to color the jellybeans.

Color Code:

4 = white	8 = green	12 = pink
5 = orange	9 = purple	13 = yellow
6 = red	10 = brown	
7 = blue	11 = black	

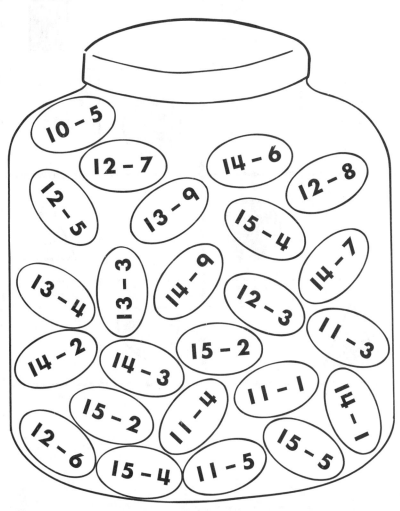

Shape Sudoku

Directions: Complete the Sudoku puzzle. Every row and column must contain a △, ▯, ♡, and ●. Do not repeat the same shape twice in any row or column.

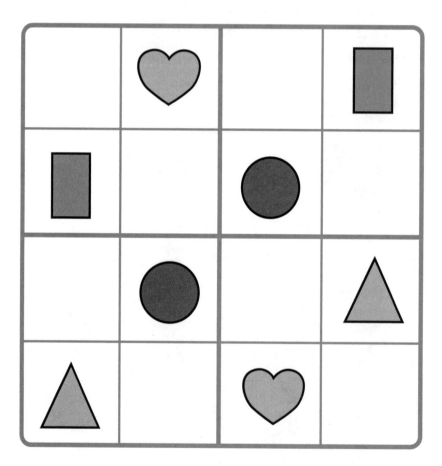

Matching Max

Directions: Find and circle the two pictures of Max that are exactly alike.

Classifying: Space Shapes

Directions: Look at the shapes. Use the code to color the picture.

Color Code:

black

red

orange

yellow

blue

green

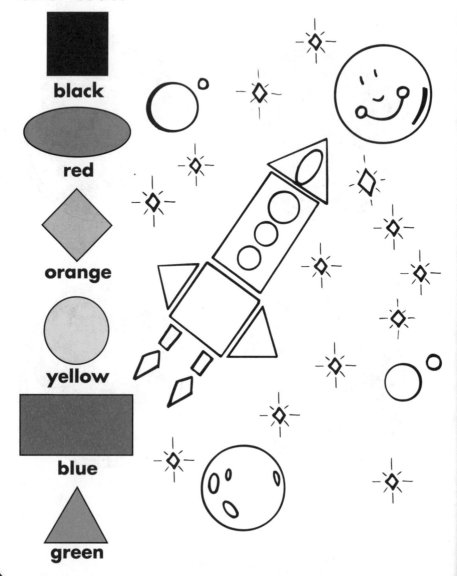

Which Is Different?

Directions: Look at the sundaes below. One is different from the others. Draw an **X** on the sundae that is different.

Subtraction: Color Code

Directions: Solve the subtraction problems. Use the code to color the picture.

Color Code:
0 = green   **2** = blue   **4** = black
1 = brown   **3** = purple   **5** = pink

Finish the Picture

Directions: The sailboat is split in half. Draw and color the other half of the sailboat to make a whole.

Hidden Picture

Directions: There are six insects hidden in the picture. Find and circle them.

ant	grasshopper	ladybug
butterfly	dragonfly	bumblebee

What Is Different?

Directions: Look at the two pictures. There are five things different in **Picture 2**. Find and circle the five things that are different in **Picture 2**.

Picture 1

Picture 2

Sudoku

Directions: Complete the Sudoku puzzle. Every row and column must contain the numbers **5**, **6**, **7**, and **8**. Do not repeat the same number twice in any row or column.

5			7
	8	6	
	5	7	
6			8

Color Code

Directions: Solve the subtraction problems. Then, color the spaces according to the answers.

Color Code:

1 = white	4 = green	7 = pink	10 = red
2 = purple	5 = yellow	8 = gray	
3 = black	6 = blue	9 = orange	

Finish the Picture

Directions: The ladybug is split in half. Draw and color the other half of the ladybug to make a whole.

Math in Science

Number Code: Gases

Have you ever poured cold water on something very hot? What happens? Steam rises off the object. The steam is a **gas**. Gas has no shape. Gases can take many shapes.

Directions: Solve the riddle to learn about gases. Add or subtract the problems. Then, use your answer and the key to write the correct letter on the line above the problem.

You see me in the sky everyday. I am made of gases. What am I?

$$\frac{\begin{array}{r} 10 \\ -8 \end{array}}{} \qquad \frac{\begin{array}{r} 5 \\ +4 \end{array}}{} \qquad \frac{\begin{array}{r} 3 \\ -2 \end{array}}{} \qquad\qquad \frac{\begin{array}{r} 7 \\ +3 \end{array}}{} \qquad \frac{\begin{array}{r} 4 \\ +4 \end{array}}{} \qquad \frac{\begin{array}{r} 12 \\ -6 \end{array}}{}$$

Key:

$\frac{E}{1}$	$\frac{H}{9}$	$\frac{S}{10}$	$\frac{T}{2}$	$\frac{U}{8}$	$\frac{N}{6}$

Classifying: Mixed Up Matter!

Directions: Help sort the liquids and solids. Cut out the pictures below. Glue each picture in the correct box.

Liquids	Solids

Graphing: Wind Direction

Use bubbles to find out which direction the wind is blowing. Then, fill in the graph. See page 84 for a quick and easy bubble recipe!

Directions: Have an adult help you find north, south, east, and west on a compass. Blow bubbles into the wind to see which direction the wind takes them. Repeat every 10 minutes and color one space for each direction the wind blows the bubbles.

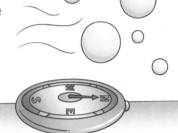

Write the Time

___ : ___				
___ : ___				
___ : ___				
	North	South	East	West

Emma's Lab

Welcome to Emma's laboratory. Use math, measurement, and science to experiment with mixing liquids, solids, and gases. This project is a real blast!

What you'll need:
- A sandwich bag (make sure there are no holes and it can seal completely)
- Paper towel
- $\frac{1}{2}$ cup white vinegar
- $1\frac{1}{2}$ tablespoons baking soda
- $\frac{1}{4}$ cup warm water
- Scissors
- Ruler
- A clear outdoor area
- An adult

What to do:

1. On a paper towel, use a ruler to draw a square that is 5 inches on each side. Then, cut it out.

2. Have an adult help you measure the baking soda and spoon it onto the paper towel. Fold the corners inward so the powder is contained in a little pouch.

3. Mix the vinegar and warm water together. Then, pour into the sandwich bag.

4. Go outside.

5. Carefully, drop the paper towel packet into the bag and seal it shut right away.

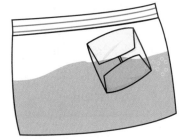

6. Shake the bag a bit. Then, put it on the ground and stand back for a surprise!

What happened to the bag? _____

The liquid vinegar and solid baking soda created a gas. There was too much gas in the bag, so it burst to let it out!

A Salty Experiment

Practice carefully measuring liquids to turn salt water into drinking water! Then, see if you can help Emma solve the problems on page 73.

What you'll need:
- $1\frac{1}{2}$ tablespoons table salt
- 3 cups water
- Mixing bowl
- Coffee cup or small bowl
- Plastic wrap
- Small rock
- An adult

What to do:

1. Have an adult help you measure 3 cups of water and pour it into the mixing bowl. Is this more or less than 1 cup of water?
   Circle one. **More** **Less**

2. Mix in $1\frac{1}{2}$ tablespoons of salt. Stir until it is dissolved.

3. Carefully, place the empty small cup into the mixing bowl. Don't let any salt water get in it! Cover the mixing bowl with plastic wrap.

4. Place a small rock in the middle of the plastic wrap, as shown. The plastic will slant slightly toward the middle where the cup is.

5. On a sunny day, put the mixing bowl outside. Soon, you will see water droplets form under the plastic and drip into the cup.

6. Wait three hours, then take the plastic off. Now, taste the water! Do you taste salt? Circle one.
   Yes **No**

Emma turns 10 cups of salt water into drinking water for a school project. Max drinks 4 cups when she is not looking. How many cups of water does Emma have left?

_____cups

If she needs 10 cups of water, how many more will she have to make after Max drank some?

_____cups

Emma's Rain Tracker

Track the rain just like Emma! Follow the directions to track how much it rains for five days. Then, use the Observation Chart on the next page to record your measurements.

What you'll need:
- One 10-inch glass or plastic container
- A handful of marbles or pebbles
- One marker
- Ruler
- An adult

What to do:

1. Place a handful of marbles or pebbles in the glass container.

2. Ask an adult to help you pour water into the container until it is 1 inch deep.

3. Draw a line where the water is with a **black** marker.

4. Place the container outside on a flat surface.

5. Ask an adult to help you use a ruler to measure the rainfall in the container each day at the same time for five days. Remember, measure starting from the **black** line you drew.

6. Track your observations on the Observation Chart!

Observation Chart

Directions: Use the chart below to write how much rain you measured every day.

Day of the Week	Rain Measurement	Draw the Weather Today
Monday		
Tuesday		
Wednesday		
Thursday		
Friday		

Halves and Wholes: Marshmallow Moons

Charting the Moon's cycle has never been tastier! Use math and marshmallows to observe the Moon every night and see its phases. This project takes a month to complete!

What you'll need:
- Bag of marshmallows
- Glue
- Construction paper
- Crayons

What to do:

1. Start observing the Moon every night at the beginning of the month.

2. Each night, go outside and look at the Moon. Does it look more like a whole circle? Or more like a half of a circle?

3. Back inside, take a bite out of a marshmallow to match the shape of the Moon you saw.

4. Glue the marshmallow to construction paper and write the date with a crayon.

5. Do this every night for a month. Make your best guess on a night it's too cloudy.

How many half Moons did you see? _____

How many whole Moons did you see? _____

Can you see a pattern throughout the month?
Circle one. **Yes   No**

Jupiter's Moon Code

Max is pretending to fly around Jupiter.

Directions: Use the code to discover the names of three of Jupiter's moons.

A	B	C	D	E	F	G	H	I	J	K	L	M
1	2	3	4	5	6	7	8	9	10	11	12	13

N	O	P	Q	R	S	T	U	V	W	X	Y	Z
14	15	16	17	18	19	20	21	22	23	24	25	26

First, Max sees Jupiter's moon named ___ ___. It has at least eight active volcanoes.
9   15

Then, he spots ___ ___ ___ ___ ___ ___ .
5   21   18   15   16   1

It is the brightest moon and covered with ice.

Next, he goes to the largest moon in the whole solar system.

It is named ___ ___ ___ ___ ___ ___ ___ ___ .
7   1   14   25   13   5   4   5

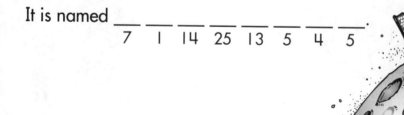

Math in Crafts

Snowy Painting

Use lots of different shapes to create this snowy scene.
See if you can name and use seven different shapes.

What you'll need:
- Dark **blue** or **black** construction paper
- Construction paper in other colors
- Thick, white tempera paint
- Small sponge
- Cotton balls
- Pie pan
- Aluminum foil
- Glue
- Scissors

What to do:

1. Cut colored construction paper into various sizes of shapes, such as: circles, squares, triangles, rectangles, ovals, rhombuses, stars, or hearts.

2. Use the shapes to create buildings and houses on the **black** or **blue** construction paper.

3. When you are satisfied with your scene, glue the paper shapes in place.

4. Cut out window shapes from aluminum foil, and glue them to the buildings.

5. Pour a small amount of white tempera paint into a pie pan.

6. Dip a sponge in the paint, and then blot the paint gently onto the paper to create snow.

7. Stretch cotton balls across the bottom of the paper to make more snow. Glue it in place.

Vegetable and Fruit Print

Use what you have learned about halves and wholes to make this tasty picture! You can create patterns or practice learning fractions while making art. Let an adult help you do the cutting.

What you'll need:
- Vegetable or fruit pieces (onions, cabbage, apples, star fruit, mushrooms, etc.)
- Tempera paint
- Pie pans or aluminum foil
- Paper
- Knife (for the adult to use)
- An adult

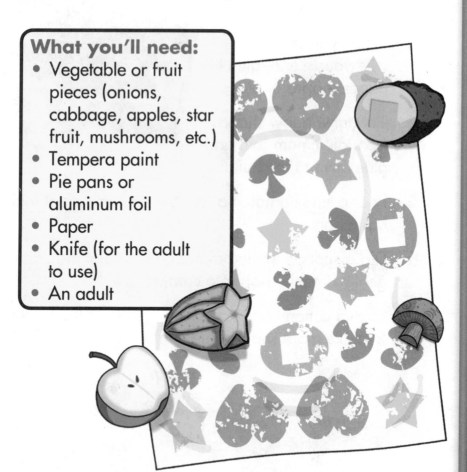

What to do:

1. Have an adult cut each vegetable or fruit in half.

2. Pour paint into the pie pans.

3. Dip the vegetable or fruit half in the paint. Blot it on scrap paper to even out the paint.

4. Stamp the vegetable or fruit half onto the paper gently. Then, lift it straight up.

5. Dip and stamp again to create a pattern.

6. Continue to stamp, experimenting with placing your stamp in different directions.

Suggestion

- Have an adult cut the fruit or vegetable into thirds (three equal parts) or fourths (four equal parts). Move the pieces around to practice learning different fractions like $\frac{1}{3}$ or $\frac{3}{4}$!

Bubbles

Use this recipe to make your own endless supply of bubbles. Test how fast you can count before all the bubbles pop!

What you'll need:

- $\frac{1}{2}$ cup glycerine (may be purchased at a pharmacy)
- $\frac{1}{2}$ cup water
- 1 tablespoon liquid dishwashing detergent
- Glass jar with a lid
- Bubble wands
- Baking pan (optional)

What to do:

1. Mix all the ingredients in a jar.

2. Make bubble wands out of twist ties, slotted spoons, clothes hangers, or straws.

3. Blow bubbles in the air and count as many as you can. Play with a friend and try counting the bubbles by twos or fives.

4. You can reuse the bubbles as long as you keep the jar tightly closed when you are finished playing.

Answer Key

6

It was a rainy day. Max and Emma could not play outside. Emma was at home in her science lab.

"Let's see how much it has rained," Emma said. "I bet my rain tracker is almost full!"

The phone rang. "Emma! Max is on the phone," her mom called.

Directions: Fill up the rain tracker. Use the ruler to color 3 inches of rain.

7

"Hi Max," Emma said.

"Hi Emma," Max said. "I put something secret in your mailbox."

"What is it?" Emma asked.

"You will see," Max said. "Once you solve it, put it in my mailbox."

"Okay, I will check now!" Emma said. She grabbed an umbrella and went outside.

Directions: Color the picture.

Colors will vary.

8

Back inside, Emma opened the letter. It was written in a secret code. "Cool!" Emma said. "Max made his own code." She looked at the key. "I see, each symbol stands for a letter," she said.

"I need to check my rain tracker first," Emma said. But it had stopped raining outside.

"I have the perfect message for Max!" Emma said as she started writing.

Directions: What will Emma do after she writes the code? Draw what happens next below.

Drawings will vary.

9

"I wish we could play outside," Max sighed. The phone rang.

"Hello?" Max said.

"Go check your mailbox!" Emma said.

"I'll go right now!" Max said.

Directions: Help Max solve the code from Emma. Use the key to unlock the message.

A	B	C	D	E	F	G	H	I	J	K	L	M

N	O	P	Q	R	S	T	U	V	W	X	Y	Z

IT STOPPED
RAINING.
LET'S PLAY
OUTSIDE.

10

Directions: Write your answers on the lines.

How many inches of rain does Emma collect on page 7?

__3__ inches

Emma got Max's message at 3:00. She put the message back in his mailbox thirty minutes later. What time does Max get her message? Draw the hands on the clock.

Use a ruler to find something around your house that measures 3 inches. Draw it below.

Drawings will vary.

Make your own rain tracker on page 74!

12

Ordinal Numbers: Birthday Balloons

Max and Emma are at a birthday party! Which balloon will they pick? Look at the balloons and follow the directions.

Drawings will vary.

Directions: Color the **second** balloon red.

Draw blue and green stripes on the **first** balloon.

Draw an animal on the **third** balloon.

Ordinal Numbers: Ice Cream Dilemma

Max and Emma love ice cream. Help them decide which ice cream cone to eat first and which to eat last.

Directions: Draw a line to the picture that matches the ordinal number in the left column.

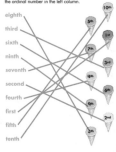

eighth
third
sixth
ninth
seventh
second
fourth
first
fifth
tenth

13

More Than

The symbol > means **more than**. It is written like this: **7 > 5**.

Directions: Count the grapes. Write the numbers on the lines. Use the symbol > to write which bunch has more.

$\underline{9} \; \gtrdot \; \underline{6}$

14

Less Than

The symbol < means **less than**. It is written like this: **6 < 7**.

Directions: Count the seeds on the watermelon. Draw less seeds on the watermelon below it.

Answers will vary.

Directions: Fill in the number of seeds you drew on the line below. Then, write the math symbol that means **less than**.

$\underline{} \; \lessdot \; 9$

15

Crazy for Bananas!

The monkeys at the zoo eat a lot of bananas. Which monkey eats more?

Directions: Count the bananas. Circle the monkey that eats more. Write the missing math symbol in the circle.

$8 \; \gtrdot \; 5$

Directions: Write the missing math symbol in each circle.

$18 \gtrdot 15$		$20 \gtrdot 12$
$4 \lessdot 6$		$2 \gtrdot 1$
$10 \gtrdot 5$		$14 \gtrdot 13$

16

Apple Addition

Addition means putting together or adding two or more numbers. When you add two numbers together, you get a **total** or **sum**.

Directions: Count the apples and write how many.

 + = $\underline{2}$

+ = $\underline{3}$

+ = $\underline{4}$

+ = $\underline{5}$

17

Addition

Directions: The key words **in all** tell you to add. Circle the key words **in all** and solve the problem.

A monster has 4 yellow shoes and 2 red shoes. How many shoes does the monster have in all?

$4 \oplus 2 = \underline{6}$

Now, draw the monster wearing all the shoes.

Drawings will vary.

18

Emma's Addition

Emma loves addition! Help Max solve the math problems she wrote for him. Then, create your own addition problem for a friend.

Directions: Add the numbers.

8	2	3	5	4
+1	+5	+7	+4	+1
9	7	10	9	5

9	5	2	5	6
+1	+3	+2	+5	+0
10	8	4	10	6

Directions: Create your own problem. Give it to a friend to solve.

_____ + _____ = _____

Answers will vary.

19

Spaceship Addition

Directions: Add the numbers. Write each answer on the spaceship.

2 + 4 =  6   1 + 3 = 4

3 + 2 = 5   5 + 1 = 6

2 + 2 = 4   6 + 2 = 8

4 + 6 = 10   2 + 7 = 9

20

Addition Problem Solving

Directions: Solve each problem. Show your work.

There are 4 🐰.
5 more 🐰 come.
Now, how many are here? __9__

$$\begin{array}{r} 4 \\ +5 \\ \hline \end{array}$$

There are 5 🍃.
There are 6 🦋.
How many 🍃 and 🦋 in all? __11__

$$\begin{array}{r} 5 \\ +6 \\ \hline \end{array}$$

Jenny has 5 🌸.
She finds 2 more 🌸.
What is the sum of 5 + 2? __7__

$$\begin{array}{r} 5 \\ +2 \\ \hline \end{array}$$

21

Subtraction

Subtraction means taking away or subtracting one number from another. The symbol used for subtraction is called a **minus sign** (–). It means to subtract the second number from the first.

Directions: Solve the number problem under each picture. Write how much fruit is left.

🍎🍎🍎🍎✗✗
5 – 2 = __3__

🟤🟤🟤🟤✗✗✗
7 – 3 = __4__

🌙✗✗
3 – 2 = __1__

🍅🍅🍅🍅🍅✗
6 – 1 = __5__

22

Butterfly Scramble

Emma wants to study butterflies in her science lab. But they keep flying away! Help catch the butterflies.

Directions: Circle the key word **left**. Write a number sentence to solve each subtraction problem.

Emma put 6 butterflies in her jar. But 2 flew out. How many butterflies are left in the jar?
__6__ – __2__ = __4__

There were 10 butterflies in a tree. Then, 9 flew into a bush. How many butterflies were left in the tree?
__10__ – __9__ = __1__

Max saw 15 butterflies. He caught 8 of them. How many butterflies does Max have left to catch?
__15__ – __8__ = __7__

Directions: Draw a picture of Max and Emma chasing the butterflies.

Drawings will vary.

23

Max's Subtraction

Max loves subtraction! Help Emma solve the math problems he wrote for her. Then, create your own subtraction problem for a friend.

Directions: Subtract to find the difference.

10	9	4	2	9
–7	–5	–3	–0	–3
3	4	1	2	6

6	8	10	7	8
–2	–6	–6	–2	–7
4	2	4	5	1

Directions: Create your own problem. Give it to a friend to solve.

_____ – _____ = _____

Answers will vary.

24

Subtraction: Pond Problems

Directions: Complete the subtraction sentences.

4 – 4 = __0__

10 – 2 = __8__

7 – 3 = __4__

6 – 5 = __1__

8 – 3 = __5__

5 – 2 = __3__

25

Subtraction Problem Solving

Directions: Solve each problem. Show your work. The first one is done for you.

There are 7.
4 swim away.
How many are left? __3__

$$\begin{array}{r} 7 \\ -4 \\ \hline \end{array}$$

Brian wants 10.
He has 3.
What is the difference? __7__

$$\begin{array}{r} 10 \\ -3 \\ \hline \end{array}$$

Marla has 8.
She gives 4 away.
What is 8 – 4? __4__

$$\begin{array}{r} 8 \\ -4 \\ \hline \end{array}$$

There are 7.
2 pop.
How many are left? __5__

$$\begin{array}{r} 7 \\ -2 \\ \hline \end{array}$$

26

Shapes and Colors

circle   triangle   square   rectangle

Directions: Color the circles blue. Color the triangles green. Color the squares purple. Color the rectangles yellow.

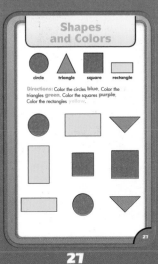

27

Classifying: Shapes

Directions: Look at the shapes. Answer the questions.

How many all white shapes? __3__

How many all green shapes? __3__

How many half green shapes? __3__

How many all green stars? __1__

How many all white circles? __1__

How many half white shapes? __3__

28

Fractions

How many equal parts? _____

Directions: Color the shapes with two equal parts.

29

Fractions: Thirds and Fourths

Directions: Each object has three equal parts. Color one part.

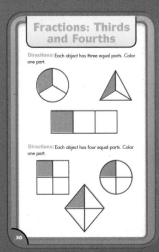

Directions: Each object has four equal parts. Color one part.

30

Cupcake Craze!

Emma wants to share eight cupcakes with four friends. If she divides the cupcakes equally, how many will everyone have?

Directions: Draw the cupcakes on the plates to show how many each of Emma's friends gets.

Drawings will vary.

31

Time: Half Hour

The little hand of the clock tells the hour. The big hand tells how many minutes after the hour. When the minute hand is on the 6, it is on the half hour. A half hour is 30 minutes. It is written :30, such as 5:30.

Directions: Look at each clock. Write the time.

_4_ : 30   _3_ : 30

_8_ : 30   _6_ : 30

_10_ : 30   _5_ : 30

32

Your Schedule

Directions: Look at the time on the clocks. Write the time. Then, draw a picture of something you do at that time.

_7_ : 30

_12_ : 00   Drawings will vary.

_5_ : 30

33

Max's Pennies

Max is counting his pennies. A penny is worth one cent. It is written 1¢.

Directions: Count Max's pennies. How many cents?

= _3_ ¢

= _8_ ¢

= _5_ ¢

= _12_ ¢

34

Count the Change

Max and Emma want to buy ice cream. Help them count their change. A nickel is worth five cents. It is written 5¢.

Directions: Count the money and write the answers.

= _4_ ¢

= _10_ ¢

= _7_ ¢

= _17_ ¢

35

Measurement: Length and Height

Directions: Use dimes to measure each object.

 _5_ dimes

_6_ dimes

_5_ dimes

_8_ dimes

_4_ dimes

36

Measurement: Weight

Emma is experimenting with weight. She is weighing objects she found in her lab. Help her find the heavier and lighter objects.

Directions: Circle the heavier object.

Directions: Circle the lighter object.

37

Picture Graph

Directions: Time to set the table! Use the picture graph to answer the questions.

How many more than ? __2__

Circle the object that is greater than .

Circle the object that is less than 🥄 🥤.

Circle the object that is equal to 🍽️.

38

Number Recognition

Directions: Use the color code to color the parrot.

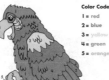

Color Code:

1 = red
2 = blue
3 = yellow
4 = green
5 = orange

40

Shape Sudoku

Directions: Complete the Sudoku puzzle. Every row and column must contain a ⬤, ⬛, ▲, and ♥. Do not repeat the same shape twice in any row or column.

41

Which Is Different?

Directions: Look at the pictures below. One is different from the others. Draw an **X** on the picture that is different.

42

Number Word Search

Directions: Find the number words zero through twelve hidden in the box. Words can be across or down.

zero	three	six	nine	twelve
one	four	seven	ten	
two	five	eight	eleven	

```
t e a z w z x a b i g t e n
o l z r b e r e v e d l a j
t w e l v e a b o n e c d z
i a r p d p s u j x e i w
c f o p l s c k i q u i i o
m s t f v i o e t t f g h d
t n u w u x g z w h g h r o
n i n e k f d f o u r t j f
a s g l q c w k o s n v m i
n y c e b o n h h p o m p y
b e x v s s e v e n w e n e
t h r e e r t a l j k x q z
m o a n e n i m u t w a y x
```

43

91

Addition and Subtraction: Crack the Code

Directions: Add or subtract the problems. Then, use your answer and the key to write the correct letter on the line above the problem. The first one is done for you.

What is an alien's favorite sweet treat?

$$\begin{array}{ccccccc} M & A & R & T & I & A & N- \\ 5 & 7 & 12 & 10 & 5 & 8 & 9 \\ +4 & +5 & -6 & -7 & +3 & +4 & -5 \\ \hline 9 & 12 & 6 & 3 & 8 & 12 & 4 \end{array}$$

$$\begin{array}{ccccccc} M & A & L & L & O & W & S! \\ 15 & 14 & 2 & 11 & 14 & 4 & 10 \\ -6 & -2 & +3 & -6 & -7 & +6 & -9 \\ \hline 9 & 12 & 5 & 5 & 7 & 10 & 1 \end{array}$$

Key:
M	A	L	S	W
9	12	5	1	10

N	R	I	T	O
4	6	8	3	7

44

Hidden Picture

Directions: There are five things hidden in Emma's lab. Find and circle them. Can you count to **100** by **5**s?

| pencil | apple | hat | candy | rock |

45

Maze

Directions: Follow the number pattern **13535** to help the fish find its home.

46

Addition: Color Code

Directions: Add to find the sum. Use the code to color the picture.

Color Code:
| 1 = red | 3 = black | 5 = brown |
| 2 = yellow | 4 = blue | 6 = green |

47

Matching Emma

Directions: Find and circle the two pictures of Emma that are exactly alike.

48

Number Search

Directions: Find the hidden numbers from the box below. They may be hidden across or down.

16177	33899	46437
37269	16396	77468
89448	97987	76373

4	6	4	3	7	1	6	3	9	6
1	3	2	5	7	8	2	6	4	1
0	3	5	1	4	2	3	9	0	8
4	8	7	1	6	1	7	7	6	2
2	9	1	7	8	3	2	8	5	7
5	9	4	9	0	2	6	1	4	6
3	1	7	3	9	7	9	8	7	3
5	2	0	2	1	4	2	6	3	7
7	8	9	4	4	8	3	4	5	3
0	4	1	6	2	3	9	2	7	1

49

Which Is Different?

Directions: Look at the aliens below. One is different from the others. Draw an **X** on the alien that is different.

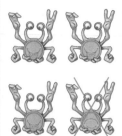

Sudoku

Directions: Complete the Sudoku puzzle. Every row and column must contain the numbers **1**, **2**, **3**, and **4**. Do not repeat the same number twice in any row or column.

2	1	4	3
4	3	1	2
1	2	3	4
3	4	2	1

50

51

Color Code: Shapes

Directions: Color the squares green, rectangles yellow, circles red, and triangles blue.

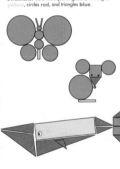

Color Code

Directions: Subtract to find the answers. Use the code to color the jellybeans.

Color Code:

4 = white	8 = green	12 = pink
5 = orange	9 = purple	13 = yellow
6 = red	10 = brown	
7 = blue	11 = black	

52

53

Shape Sudoku

Directions: Complete the Sudoku puzzle. Every row and column must contain a △, ▮, ♥, and ●. Do not repeat the same shape twice in any row or column.

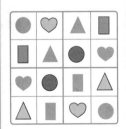

Matching Max

Directions: Find and circle the two pictures of Max that are exactly alike.

54

55

Classifying: Space Shapes

Directions: Look at the shapes. Use the code to color the picture.

Color Code:

black
red
orange
yellow
blue
green

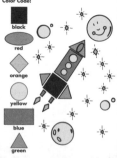

56

Which Is Different?

Directions: Look at the sundaes below. One is different from the others. Draw an **X** on the sundae that is different.

57

Subtraction: Color Code

Directions: Solve the subtraction problems. Use the code to color the picture.

Color Code:

| 0 = green | 2 = blue | 4 = black |
| 1 = brown | 3 = purple | 5 = pink |

58

Finish the Picture

Directions: The sailboat is split in half. Draw and color the other half of the sailboat to make a whole.

59

Hidden Picture

Directions: There are six insects hidden in the picture. Find and circle them.

| ant | grasshopper | ladybug |
| butterfly | dragonfly | bumblebee |

60

What Is Different?

Directions: Look at the two pictures. There are five things different in **Picture 2**. Find and circle the five things that are different in **Picture 2**.

Picture 1

Picture 2

61

Sudoku

Directions: Complete the Sudoku puzzle. Every row and column must contain the numbers **5**, **6**, **7**, and **8**. Do not repeat the same number twice in any row or column.

5	6	8	7
7	8	6	5
8	5	7	6
6	7	5	8

Color Code

Directions: Solve the subtraction problems. Then, color the spaces according to the answers.

Color Code:
1 = white	4 = green	7 = pink	10 = red
2 = purple	5 = yellow	8 = gray	
3 = black	6 = blue	9 = orange	

Finish the Picture

Directions: The ladybug is split in half. Draw and color the other half of the ladybug to make a whole.

Number Code: Gases

Have you ever poured cold water on something very hot? What happens? Steam rises off the object. The steam is a **gas**. Gas has no shape. Gases can take many shapes.

Directions: Solve the riddle to learn about gases. Add or subtract the problems. Then, use your answer and the key to write the correct letter on the line above the problem.

You see me in the sky everyday. I am made of gases. What am I?

$$
\underset{\begin{array}{c}10\\-8\\\hline 2\end{array}}{T}\ \underset{\begin{array}{c}5\\+4\\\hline 9\end{array}}{H}\ \underset{\begin{array}{c}3\\-2\\\hline 1\end{array}}{E}\qquad\underset{\begin{array}{c}7\\+3\\\hline 10\end{array}}{S}\ \underset{\begin{array}{c}4\\+4\\\hline 8\end{array}}{U}\ \underset{\begin{array}{c}12\\-6\\\hline 6\end{array}}{N}
$$

Key:	E	H	S	T	U	N
	1	9	10	2	8	6

Classifying: Mixed Up Matter!

Directions: Help sort the liquids and solids. Cut out the pictures below. Glue each picture in the correct box.

Liquids	Solids

Graphing: Wind Direction

Use bubbles to find out which direction the wind is blowing. Then, fill in the graph. See page 84 for a quick and easy bubble recipe!

Directions: Have an adult help you find north, south, east, and west on a compass. Blow bubbles into the wind to see which direction the wind takes them. Repeat every 10 minutes and color one space for each direction the wind blows the bubbles.

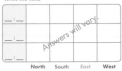

Write the Time

	North	South	East	West
__:__				
__:__				
__:__				

Answers will vary.

Card 71

What to do:

1. On a paper towel, use a ruler to draw a square that is 5 inches on each side. Then, cut it out.

2. Have an adult help you measure the baking soda and spoon it onto the paper towel. Fold the corners inward so the powder is contained in a little pouch.

3. Mix the vinegar and warm water together. Then, pour into the sandwich bag.

4. Go outside.

5. Carefully, drop the paper towel packet into the bag and seal it shut right away.

6. Shake the bag a bit. Then, put it on the ground and stand back for a surprise!

What happened to the bag? __The bag burst.__

> The liquid vinegar and solid baking soda created a gas. There was too much gas in the bag, so it burst to let it out!

71

Card 73

What to do:

1. Have an adult help you measure 3 cups of water and pour it into the mixing bowl. Is this more or less than 1 cup of water? Circle one. **More** Less

2. Mix in 1½ tablespoons of salt. Stir until it is dissolved.

3. Carefully, place the empty small cup into the mixing bowl. Don't let any salt water get in it! Cover the mixing bowl with plastic wrap.

4. Place a small rock in the middle of the plastic wrap, as shown. The plastic will slant slightly toward the middle where the cup is.

5. On a sunny day, put the mixing bowl outside. Soon, you will see water droplets form under the plastic and drip into the cup.

6. Wait three hours, then take the plastic off. Now, taste the water! Do you taste salt? Circle one. Yes No __Answers will vary.__

Emma turns 10 cups of salt water into drinking water for a school project. Max drinks 4 cups when she is not looking. How many cups of water does Emma have left?

__6__ cups

If she needs 10 cups of water, how many more will she have to make after Max drank some?

__4__ cups

73

Card 75

Observation Chart

Directions: Use the chart below to write how much rain you measured every day.

Day of the Week	Rain Measurement	Draw the Weather Today
Monday		
Tuesday		
Wednesday		
Thursday		
Friday		

Answers will vary.

75

Card 77

What to do:

1. Start observing the Moon every night at the beginning of the month.

2. Each night, go outside and look at the Moon. Does it look more like a whole circle? Or more like a half of a circle?

3. Back inside, take a bite out of a marshmallow to match the shape of the Moon you saw.

4. Glue the marshmallow to construction paper and write the date with a crayon.

5. Do this every night for a month. Make your best guess on a night it's too cloudy.

How many half Moons did you see? __Answers__

How many whole Moons did you see? __will vary.__

Can you see a pattern throughout the month? Circle one. **Yes** No

77

Card 78

Jupiter's Moon Code

Max is pretending to fly around Jupiter.

Directions: Use the code to discover the names of three of Jupiter's moons.

A	B	C	D	E	F	G	H	I	J	K	L	M
1	2	3	4	5	6	7	8	9	10	11	12	13

N	O	P	Q	R	S	T	U	V	W	X	Y	Z
14	15	16	17	18	19	20	21	22	23	24	25	26

First, Max sees Jupiter's moon named __I O__. It has
at least eight active volcanoes.   9   15

Then, he spots __E U R O P A__
5 21 18 15 16 1

It is the brightest moon and covered with ice.

Next, he goes to the largest moon in the whole solar system.

It is named __G A N Y M E D E__
7   1 14 25 13 5   4   5

78